RWD-14 "Czapla"

In 1933, at the Experimental Aviation Workshops, a preliminary project for an observation aircraft (then known as a "companion aircraft"), the RWD-12, was created on the order of the military aviation. The RWD-12 was similar to the RWD-8, and was to be powered by a Wright 220 HP engine. The project was not accepted and was not realized, as it was considered to offer too little improvement over existing designs. It was replaced by the S. Rogalski and J. Drzewiecki RWD-14 project from 1934 and 1935, in which S. Krowacki also participated. Competitors to the RWD-14 included the R-XXI project and the PWS U-6 and Z-7 projects – rejected by the military.

In 1935, a prototype of the RWD-14 (factory number 118) was built, equipped with a Pratt-Whitney Wasp TB 400 HP engine. The RWD-14 prototype was flown for the first time in December 1935 or early 1936 by A. Onoszko at the Okęcie Airport in Warsaw. In the initial flights, A. Onoszko observed the automatic opening of the slot segment over the canopy and its retraction at high angles of attack, such as during landing, leading to the removal of this slot segment. The aircraft underwent factory trials in the first half of 1936 and flight tests at the ITL in June. These tests revealed that it achieved a high maximum speed of 251 km/h, but it had a narrow undercarriage and the fuel tank was difficult to replace, necessitating modifications. The prototype underwent suitability tests at the ITL in September, October, and December 1936, and returned to the manufacturer in early April 1937. According to a comparison from December 7, 1936, the aircraft was calculated and technically expected to have: a total weight of 1400 kg (actual weight was 1620 kg), a payload of 310 kg (actual payload was 225 kg), a maximum speed of 270 km/h (achieved 251 km/h), a ceiling of 7200 m (achieved 4000 m), and a range of 380 km (achieved 350 km).

In August 1936, the Aviation Command ordered a second prototype of the RWD-14a (RWD-14/II), planning to use the PZSkoda G-1620bis engine. The task of improving the aircraft was assigned to Bronisław Żurakowski. He redesigned the fuselage truss, replacing carbon steel tubes with chrome-molybdenum steel tubes and replacing wire bracing with rod bracing from tubes, thus reducing the structure's weight. He also modified the wing fittings and struts, allowing for the wings to be folded. The undercarriage was widened by changing its layout; the shock absorbers were supported upwards to the fuselage, as in the RWD-8. The fuel tank, originally located under the pilot's feet, was replaced with a tank occupying the entire height of the front fuselage. Żurakowski designed the enclosure for the Polish G-1620 A Mors engine, but when this engine was damaged during bench tests, the aircraft was fitted with a Wasp SB engine instead.

The documentation for this version was prepared in the fall of 1936, and based on it, the second and then a third prototype, designated RWD-14a, were built in the winter of 1936/37. The second prototype RWD-14/II (factory number 134), still without its canvas covering, was presented to the military on December 12, 1936, and made its maiden flight in January 1937. On April 20, 1937, ITL test pilot Roland Kalpas, unable to recover the second prototype from a dive, bailed out with a parachute, and the aircraft crashed. It was determined that the aircraft had insufficient tail construction.

Technical specifications for the third prototype were developed at the ITL (Institute of Aviation Technology) between May 31 and July 3, 1937. In response to ITL's request, the tail structure of the third prototype was redesigned from a single-spar to a double-spar configuration to strengthen its construction. This aircraft was equipped with a G-1620B engine. The RWD-14/III (factory number 145) was flown by E. Przysiecki at the beginning of 1938. The aircraft was handed over for testing at ITL on January 20.

The aircraft met the requirement of diving flight at a speed 15% higher than its maximum, but the ITL demanded that it achieve a dive speed 30% higher than its maximum. This demand was protested by the designers, but ITL insisted on conducting

The first prototype – RWD-14/I. (Andrzej Glass)

such a test. During the dive test on the third prototype, the same difficulties with recovery from the dive were encountered. Pilot E. Przysiecki had to bail out with a parachute, and the aircraft subsequently crashed. After extensive investigations, the cause of the accidents was found. It turned out that at high speeds, the fuselage truss was deforming, and when the control stick was released, one of the levers in the control system would catch on a rod of the fuselage truss. As a result, the aircraft became uncontrollable in a dive, accelerating until it disintegrated in the air.

These issues with the prototypes delayed the completion of the aircraft's trials by two years.

The fourth prototype, RWD-14b (RWD-14/IV), featured a strengthened rear fuselage and an improved control system kinematics. It was powered by the G-1620B Mors B engine and was flown by E. Przysiecki in the first half of 1938. The prototype underwent suitability trials at the ITL from July 19 to August 18, 1938, and started operational trials on September 5, 1938. In 1938, the revised documentation for the RWD-14b was handed over to the Lublin Aircraft Factory (LWS) in exchange for the Aviation Command covering the costs of the prototype work.

At LWS, the production preparation of this aircraft was overseen by engineer R. Bartel, the implementation of design changes was managed by engineer R. Aleksandrowicz (acting as a liaison with the DWL), and the technological preparation was handled by engineer Jan Luboiński. LWS started the production of the RWD-14b series in 1938. The aircraft received the military designation "Czapla" (Heron) and the military number 55, which was previously assigned to the PZL Ł.2, already retired from service.

The serially produced aircraft differed from the prototype in several ways: they had a tail wheel with a shock absorber instead of a skid, the slots were fitted with dampers, and the method of folding the wings was modified. In one of the aircraft, a segmented extendable windscreen for the second cockpit was tested, aiming to better protect the observer. The production of "Czapla" ended on February 28, 1939, with a total of 65 serial aircraft built. The cost of the airframe was 46,000 złoty, the

The RWD-14b "Czapla" in tests at the ITL in 1938. The aircraft differs from the production version. (Andrzej Glass)

The RWD-14b with folded wings. (Andrzej Glass)

engine 50,000 złoty, equipment and armament 7,000 złoty, and the radio station 7,000 złoty, totalling 110,000 złoty.

The RWD-14 "Czapla" had short take-off and landing characteristics, similar to the RWD-9 and RWD-13 aircraft. However, due to its prolonged development period, by the time it entered service, it was somewhat outdated, especially since the production of the modern LWS-3 "Mewa" aircraft, intended for a similar role, began in 1939. "Czapla" and "Mewa" were intended to replace the R-XIII aircraft in observation squadrons (formerly known as companion squadrons).

In the spring and summer of 1939, the "Czapla" was used to rearm the observation squadrons: 13th Observation Squadron in the 1st Aviation Regiment in Warsaw, 23rd O.S. in the 2nd A.R. in Krakow, 33rd O.S. in the 3rd A.R. in Poznan, 53rd O.S. in the 5th A.R. in Lida, and 63rd O.S. in the 6th A.R. in Lviv. Each squadron received 7 "Czaplas", totaling 35 aircraft. The remaining 30 "Czaplas" were kept in reserve. At the end of August 1939, these squadrons were transferred from their regiments to the aviation units of various armies: the 13th O.S. to the Independent Operational Group "Narew", the 63rd O.S. to the Army "Łódź", the 33rd O.S. to the Army "Poznań", the 53rd O.S. to the Army "Modlin", and the 23rd O.S. to the Army "Kraków". These units fought with the "Czapla" during the September 1939 war. During the war, 14 "Czaplas" were received by the squadrons as reinforcements. 35 "Czaplas" were destroyed during military operations, and being a new, unknown type, they were also shot down by friendly forces. 17 "Czaplas" were evacuated to Romania (where they were used by the Romanian air force for observer training during the war), and 12 to Latvia.

Before the war, no photographs of the RWD-14 were published, and its name was not mentioned in the press. They were included in the aircraft's manual, which was classified. As a result, the German and Soviet air forces had no information about this aircraft in their aircraft recognition manuals and were surprised by the existence of the "Czapla". For the same reason, the number of Polish photographs of this aircraft is limited.

Construction

The RWD-14 "Czapla" was a two-seat observation aircraft with a mixed construction and a strut-braced high-wing configuration with fixed landing gear. Here's a detailed breakdown of its construction:

- Fuselage: The fuselage had an oval cross-section, featuring a lattice structure welded from chrome-molybdenum steel tubes. It was covered with canvas on a wooden slat frame. The front of the fuselage, behind the engine, was covered with aluminium sheet.
- Cockpit: It was a two-seat, open cockpit, shielded in front by windscreens. The instrument panel in the front cockpit included an airspeed indicator with turn indicator (so-called flight controller), altimeter, variometer, compass, longitudinal inclinometer, tachometer, thermometer, oil thermometer, fuel pressure gauge, clock, and fuel gauge. The aircraft had dual controls (removable control stick in the observer's cockpit). Brake levers were located on the control column.
- Equipment: The equipment included a fire extinguisher, first aid kit, navigation lights, and a retractable landing spotlight (under the fuselage). The aircraft was adapted for installing an N2L/T or Ava N2L/O radio station and a photographic camera. Steps were provided on the left side of the fuselage.

- Landing Gear: The main landing gear was of a tricycle type, with Avia 50300PBT oil-air shock absorbers and Dunlop low-pressure tires with Bendix brakes. The wheel track was 3.12 meters. The self-aligning tail wheel had a Dowty shock absorber and was faired.
- Wing: The wing was rectangular with a slight sweep, three-part, wooden, and double-sparred. It was plywood-covered up to the first spar and then covered with canvas. It featured three-part automatic wooden slots and could be folded backward for storage (width after folding – 3.9 meters). The wing was supported on the fuselage by a steel tube cabane and braced by steel tube V-struts. The wing profile was IAW 192, and it had slotted ailerons. A mount for two illumination rockets was present on the right wing.
- Tail Unit: The tail unit was wooden, with plywood-covered stabilizers and canvas-covered control surfaces. The horizontal stabilizer was adjustable and supported by struts.

This construction offered a blend of strength, lightweight, and functionality, making the RWD-14 "Czapla" suitable for observation and reconnaissance roles.

The RWD-14 "Czapla" was armed with the following weaponry:

1. Observer's Gun: A 7.92 mm Vickers F machine gun, which was a movable gun operated by the observer. It was equipped with 5 magazines, each containing 97 rounds.
2. Pilot's Gun: A 7.92 mm PWU wz. 33 machine gun, fixed and firing forward through the propeller arc, synchronized with a JS 38 synchronizer. It had a total ammunition reserve of 500 rounds.

The aircraft was powered by a PZL G-1620 B Mors II engine, which was an air-cooled, nine-cylinder radial engine. It had a take-off power of 470 HP and a nominal power of 430 HP at 2150 rpm, weighing 290 kg. The engine mount was welded from steel tubes. The engine was covered with a ring-shaped aluminium shroud, and there was a ring-shaped exhaust collector behind the engine. The propeller was a two-blade, fixed, wooden Szomański model. The aircraft had a fuel tank capacity of 315 litres in the front of the fuselage, behind the engine, and an oil tank capacity of 31 litres. The average fuel consumption was about 105 litres per hour.

Paint scheme:

Indeed, the limited number of RWD-14 "Czapla" aircraft that were delivered to combat units before the outbreak of World War II has resulted in sparse iconographic documentation. This scarcity makes it challenging to accurately reconstruct the complete painting schemes of these aircraft. The available records and photographs are limited, leading to some uncertainty and reliance on a few documented examples or surviving aircraft for understanding their exact appearance and coloration. This scarcity of information is a common issue for many military vehicles and equipment from that era, particularly those that saw limited production or deployment.

The top of the aircraft was painted khaki. The underside was silver.

Polish Air Force Markings: Small, asymmetrically placed checkerboards were on the upper wing surfaces. The most well-documented example, tested at ITL, had a white-painted rudder.

Serial Numbers: Aircraft delivered to units had the type designation (55) and serial number painted in black on the left side of the fuselage towards the rear. The lower wing surfaces had a so-called "police number" consisting of a letter and numbers. Known iconography shows such markings for aircraft with numbers 2 and 3.

Tactical Numbers: Other known photos, especially those of the 23rd Observation Squadron, show white tactical numbers painted on the fuselage. For the aircraft with the tactical number 5, there's a cut-out just behind this number, likely indicating the placement of the squadron's emblem within a square.

The rudder carried the LWS manufacturer's mark.

Romanian Air Force RWD-14s initially retained the Polish colour scheme. Polish markings were painted over with similar colours, and then Romanian air force insignias were added. Small tactical numbers were painted on the rudder. After the attack on the USSR, yellow identification stripes (on the fuselage and wings) were added for quick identification.

RWD-14b "Czapla," CWL Dęblin, probably spring 1939. (MLP)

A high-quality photograph of the RWD-14b "Czapla" aircraft. Visible details include the engine cowling and folded wings.
(Marek Rogusz)

A burned RWD-14b "Czapla" observation aircraft from the 33rd Observation Squadron. The letter "P" under the wing confirms the aircraft's affiliation with the 3rd Air Regiment. (Marek Rogusz)
Below: The same "Czapla" after further destruction. (Tomasz J. Kopański)

The RWD-14b "Czapla" aircraft, no. 5, from the 23rd Observation Squadron, abandoned somewhere along the unit's combat route. The engine cowling is placed at the rear of the fuselage. (Tomasz J. Kopański)

The Breguet 19 aircraft, no. 44. To the right, an LWS "Czapla," no. 55-39.
(Roman Postek)

Hptm. Kraemer, Gef. Mühlenberg, and Uffz. Zhivel in a Mercedes with the "Czapla" 55-39 in the background. The LWS logo is clearly visible on the tail. In the background, the Breguet 19, no. 44. (Stratus)

The RWD-14b "Czapla" aircraft, no. 3, from the 23rd Observation Squadron in German hands.
(Marek Rogusz)

RWD-14b "Czapla," no. 37 (formerly 55.37), from the Şcoala de Perfecţionare in Tecuci, featuring standard markings from 1942: King Michael's crosses, a tricolour band on the rudder, and a yellow band around the fuselage.

An olive-green RWD-14b aircraft with a light greyish-blue underside from the Şcoala de Perfecţionare in Tecuci in 1942.

A photograph of the RWD-14b, no. 56, from the Centrul de Instrucţie al Aeronauticii in Buzău in 1944, clearly showing details of the wing mounting, undercarriage structure, and engine cowling.

15 July 1944, Şcoala de Tir şi Bombardament in Mamaia. The total destruction caused by the Soviet army also affected the RWD-14b, no. 40, from which the fabric covering of the fuselage was torn away, revealing structural details.

The crash of the RWD-14b, no. 138 (1943), at the Şcoala de Perfecţionare in Tecuci. The standard placement of all marking elements is clearly visible.

Rys. 1. 1 L i 1 P.   Przedział pilota

1. Mapnik
2. Dźwignia kurka paliwowego
3. Koło regulacji statecznika wysokości
4. Zawór blokujący hamulce
5. Orczyk
6. Przekaźnik hamulca
7. Dźwignia regulatora składu mieszanki
8. Dźwignia sterowania przepustnicy
9. Pasek do umocowania orczyka
10. Dźwignia unieruchomienia silnika
11. Przełącznik iskrowników
12. Uchwyt do umocowania drążka sterowego
13. Termostat
14. Manometr oleju
15. Ramka dla wykresu kompensacji busoli
16. Manometr paliwa
17. Termometr oleju
18. Obrotomierz
19. Kontroler lotu
20. Busola
21. Chyłomierz podłużny
22. Wariometr
23. Wysokościomierz
24. Zegarek czasowy
25. Paliwomierz
26. Uchwyt ładowniczy k.m.
27. Przekaźnik giętki paliwomierza
28. Pompka zastrzykowa
29. Regulator napięcia
30. Drążek sterowy
31. Dźwignia wyrzutowa rac
32. Gaśnica
33. Tablica rozdzielcza
34. Dźwignia regulacji fotela
35. Bezpieczniki zapasowe
36. Pasy bezpieczeństwa
37. Cięgło przysłony silnika

Widok ogólny

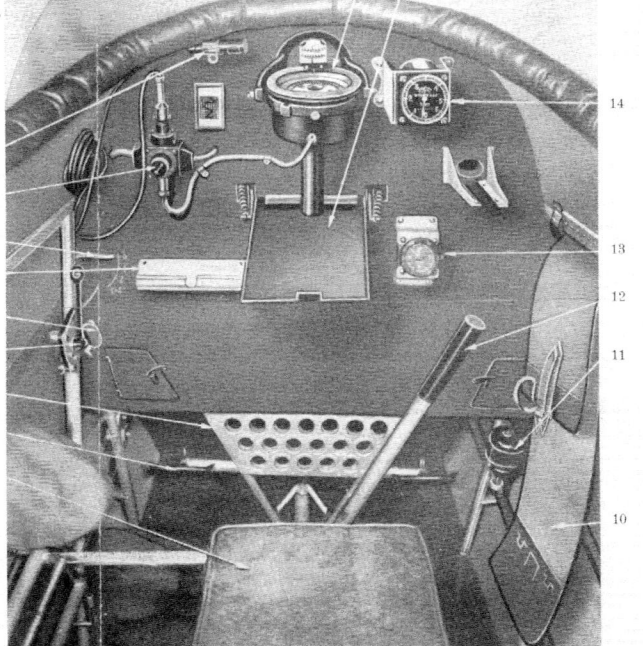

Rys. 2.   Przednia ściana przedziału obserwatora

1. Lampa kabinowa
2. Opornik przyciemniający
3. Dźwignia przełącznika iskrowników
4. Piórnik
5. Obsada pistoletu sygnałowego
6. Dźwignia sterowania przepustnicy
7. Skrzynka naboi sygnałowych
8. Orczyk obserwatora
9. Krzesełko składane
10. Pas mocujący spadochron
11. Gaśnica
12. Drążek sterowy
13. Zegarek czasowy
14. Wysokościomierz
15. Stolik
16. Busola

Photos and drawings from the Aircraft Maintenance Manual.
(Tomasz J. Kopański)

37   7   8   11

10

9

6

5

1   3

Lewa ściana

Pilot's cockpit.

28   31   32   33   35

34

Prawa ściana

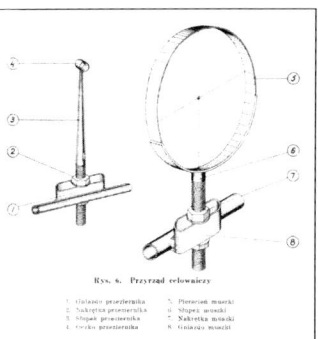

Rys. 7. Umieszczenie tablicy rozdzielczej w przedziale pilota

6. Regulator napięcia
7. Tablica rozdzielcza pilota
9. Tabliczka rozgałęźna 4-ro zaciskowa
10. Lampa busoli pilota
11. Lampa kabinowa oświetlająca tablicę przyrządów pokładowych
28. Wyrzutnik rac oświetlających

Rys. 1. Stanowisko obserwatora

1. Magazynek
2. K. m. Vickers obs.
3. Przeziernik
4. Gniazdo k. m.
5. Muszka wiatrowa
6. Wózek podstawy
7. Półpierścień podstawy
8. Pochwa sprężyny kompensacyjnej
9. Czop na magazynek
10. Worek na łuski

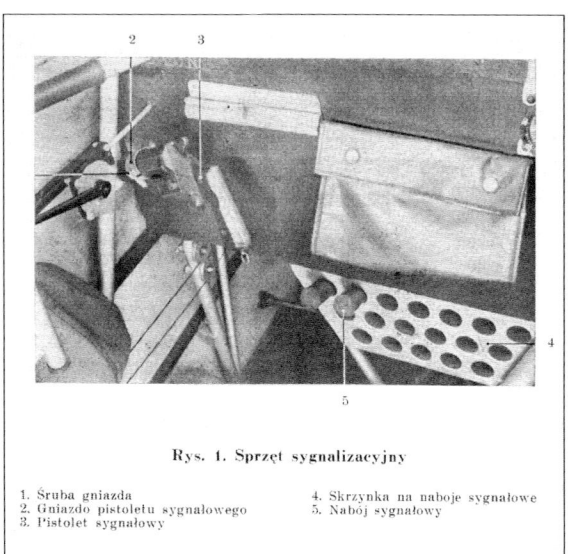

Rys. 1. Sprzęt sygnalizacyjny

1. Śruba gniazda
2. Gniazdo pistoletu sygnałowego
3. Pistolet sygnałowy
4. Skrzynka na naboje sygnałowe
5. Nabój sygnałowy

Above: Fig. 1 Signaling Equipment.
Above, right: Fig. 5 Fuel Valve Placement.

Rys. 5. Umieszczenie kurka paliwowego

1. Korek spustowy zbiornika
2. Kurek paliwowy
3. Reflektor sygnalizacyjny

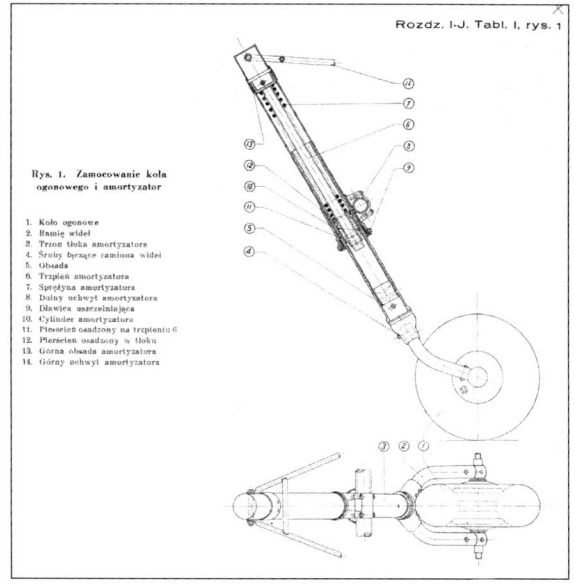

Rozdz. I-J. Tabl. I, rys. 1

Rys. 1. Zamocowanie koła ogonowego i amortyzator

1. Koło ogonowe
2. Ramię wideł
3. Trzon tłoka amortyzatora
4. Śruby łączące ramiona wideł
5. Obsada
6. Trzpień amortyzatora
7. Sprężyna amortyzatora
8. Dolny uchwyt amortyzatora
9. Dławica uszczelniająca
10. Cylinder amortyzatora
11. Pierścień osadzony na trzpieniu 6
12. Pierścień osadzony w tłoku
13. Górna obsada amortyzatora
14. Górny uchwyt amortyzatora

Tailwheel Mounting and Shock Absorber

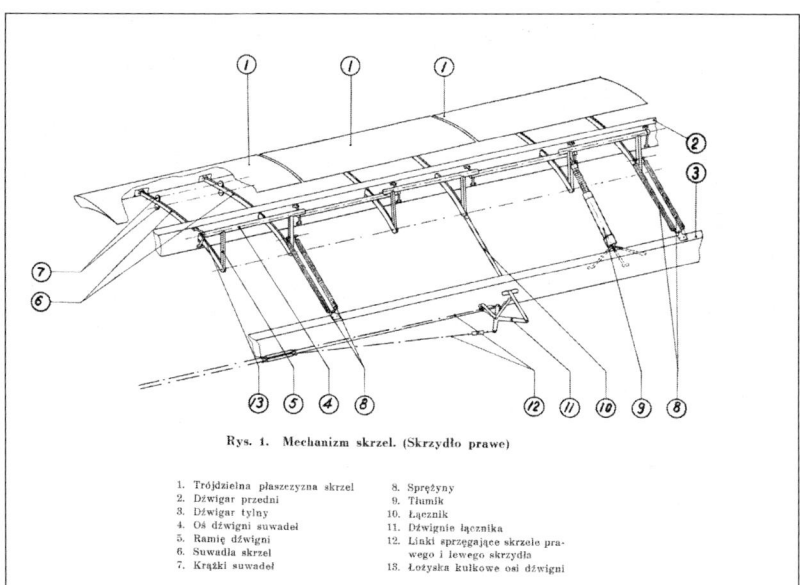

Rys. 1. Mechanizm skrzel. (Skrzydło prawe)

1. Trójdzielna płaszczyzna skrzel
2. Dźwigar przedni
3. Dźwigar tylny
4. Oś dźwigni suwadeł
5. Ramię dźwigni
6. Suwadła skrzel
7. Krążki suwadeł
8. Sprężyny
9. Tłumik
10. Łącznik
11. Dźwignie łącznika
12. Linki sprzęgające skrzele prawego i lewego skrzydła
13. Łożyska kulkowe osi dźwigni

Wing mechanization, starboard wing.

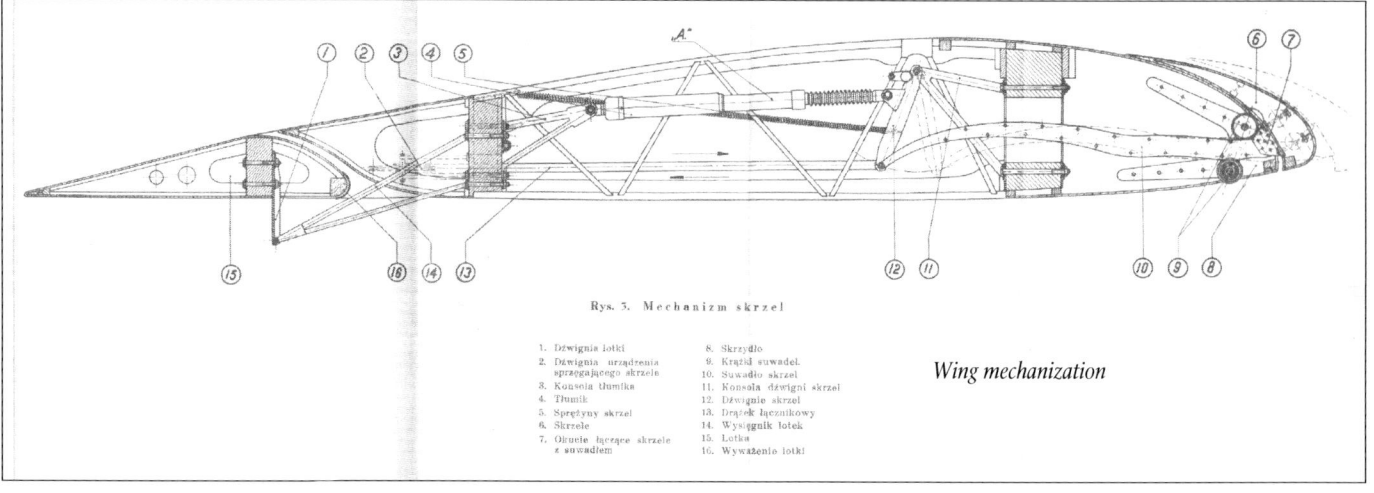

Rys. 3. Mechanizm skrzel

1. Dźwignia lotki
2. Dźwignia urządzenia sprzęgającego skrzele
3. Konsola tłumika
4. Tłumik
5. Sprężyny skrzel
6. Skrzele
7. Ogniwo łączące skrzele z suwadłem
8. Skrzydło
9. Krążki suwadeł
10. Suwadło skrzel
11. Konsola dźwigni skrzel
12. Dźwignie skrzel
13. Drążek łącznikowy
14. Wysięgnik lotek
15. Lotka
16. Wyważenie lotki

Wing mechanization

Rys. 8. Umieszczenie uchwytu rac oświetlających

13. Lampa pozycyjna prawa
26. Drzwiczki komory rac
16. Uchwyt rac oświetlających wraz ze stykami elektrycznymi zapalania

Rys. 9. Przedział obserwatora — Umieszczenie lampy kabinowej

19. Opornik przyciemniający
20. Gniazdo lampy kabinowej obs.
21. Lampa kabinowa przenośna obs.
24. Gniazdo lampy busoli
30. Trzymak przewodu
31. Trzymak lampy

Rys. 6. Umieszczenie regulatora napięcia

5. Filtr przeciwzakłóceniowy regulatorowy
6. Regulator napięcia

Rys. 1. Przednia część kadłuba samolotu

1. Dźwignia ładownicza
2. K. m. lot. wz. 36
3. Osłona ogniowa
4. Drzwiczki do wyjmowania łusek i ogniwek

Rys. 5. Skrzynki i przewody nabojowe

1. Skrzynka nabojowa
2. Pokrywa skrzynki nabojowej
3. Pokrywka przewodu doprowadzającego
4. Przewód odprowadzający ogniwka
5. Przewód doprowadzający naboje
6. Przewód odprowadzający łuski
7. Tylna podpora k. m.
8. Skrzynka zbiorcza na łuski i ogniwka
9. Śruba wspornika skrzynki nabojowej
10. Wspornik skrzynki nabojowej

Fig. 8 Placement of Illuminating Flares.
Fig. 9 Observer's Compartment.
Fig. 6 Placement of the Voltage Regulator.
Fig. 1 Forward fuselage section of the aircraft.
Fig. 5 Ammunition boxes and feed chutes.

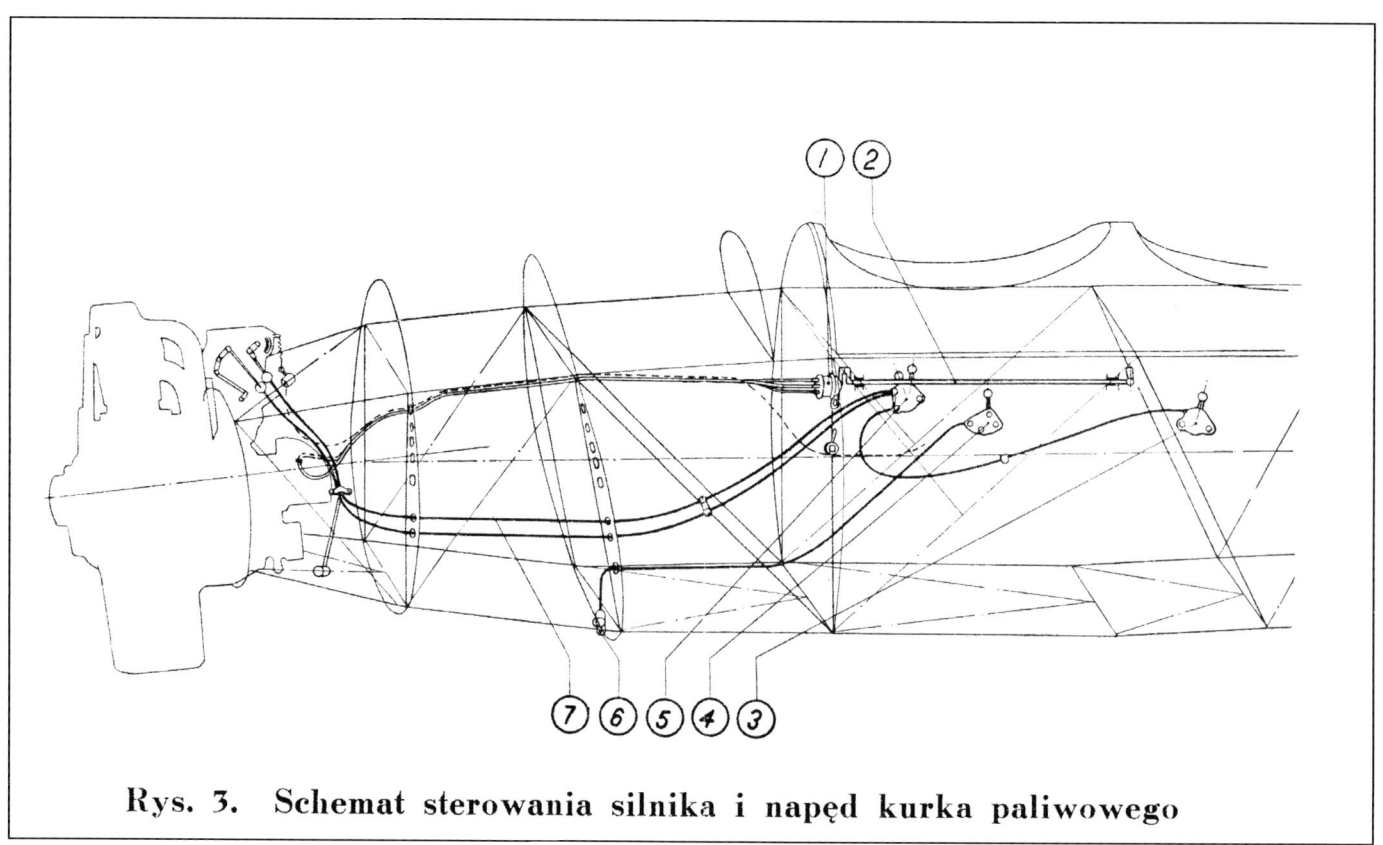

Rys. 3. Schemat sterowania silnika i napęd kurka paliwowego

Fig. 3. Engine Control and Fuel Valve Drive Diagram

1. *Magneto switch*
2. *Magneto switch rod*
3. *Throttle control lever in the observer's compartment*
4. *Fuel valve lever*
5. *Throttle and mixture control levers in the pilot's compartment*
6. *Fuel valve*
7. *Flexible linkages*

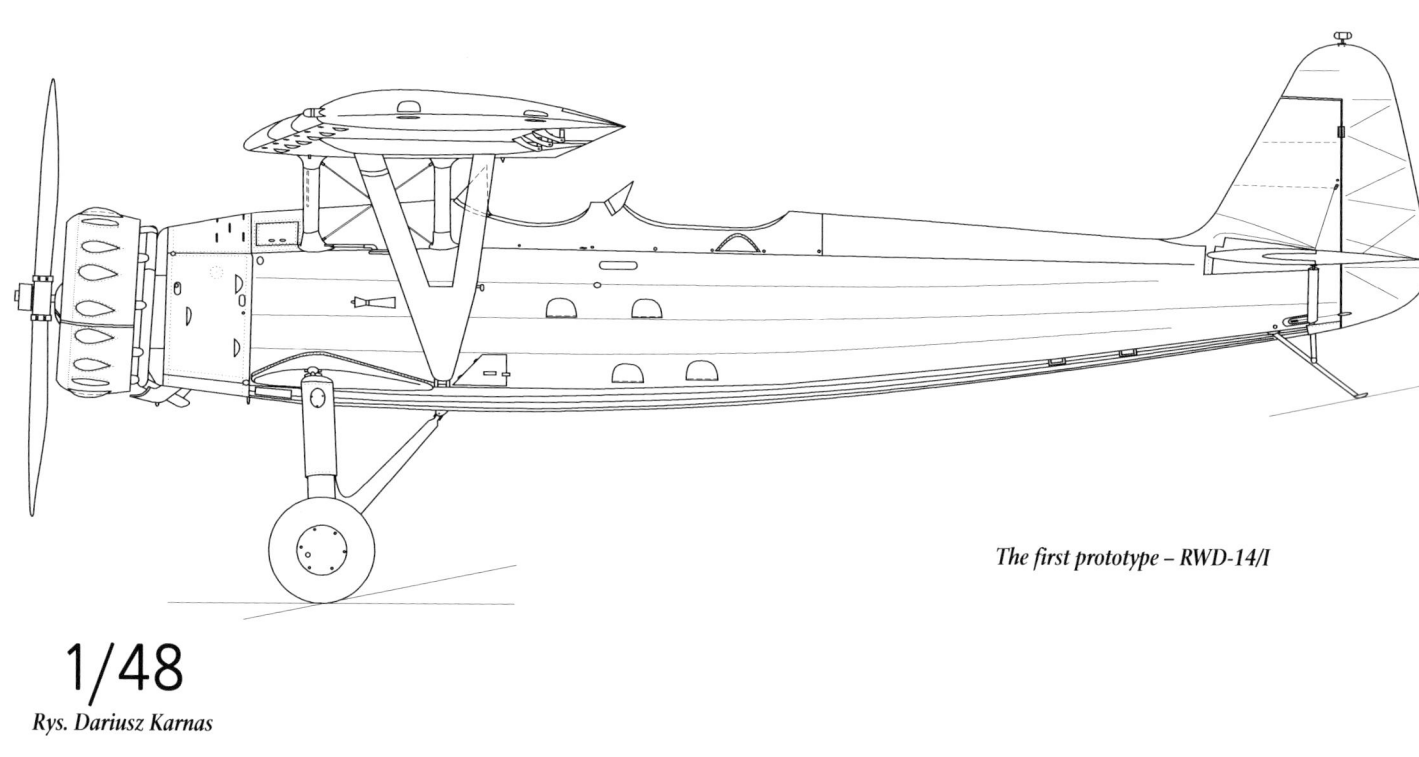

The first prototype – RWD-14/I

1/48

Rys. Dariusz Karnas

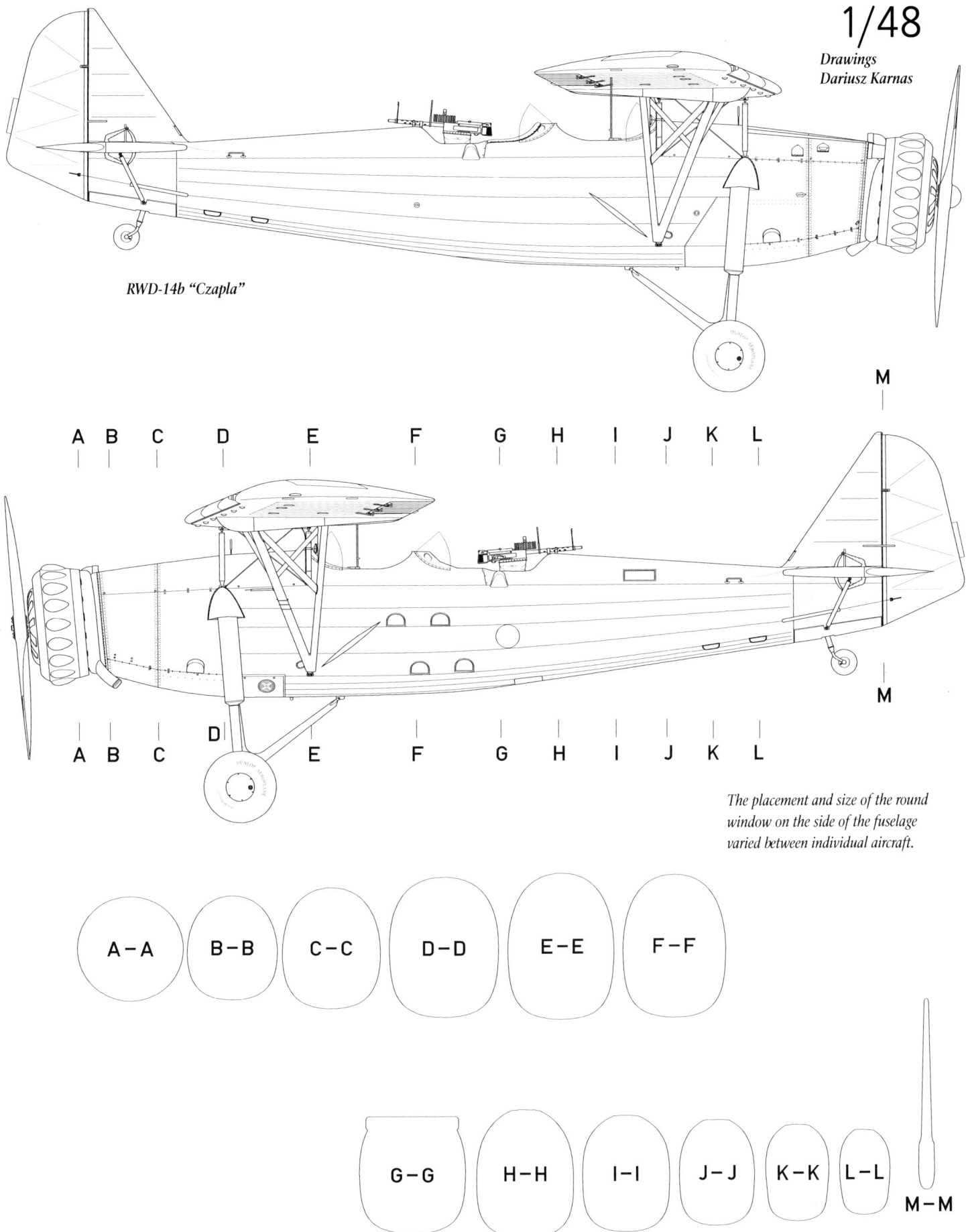

1/48

*Drawings
Dariusz Karnas*

RWD-14b "Czapla"

The placement and size of the round
window on the side of the fuselage
varied between individual aircraft.

A–A B–B C–C D–D E–E F–F

G–G H–H I–I J–J K–K L–L M–M

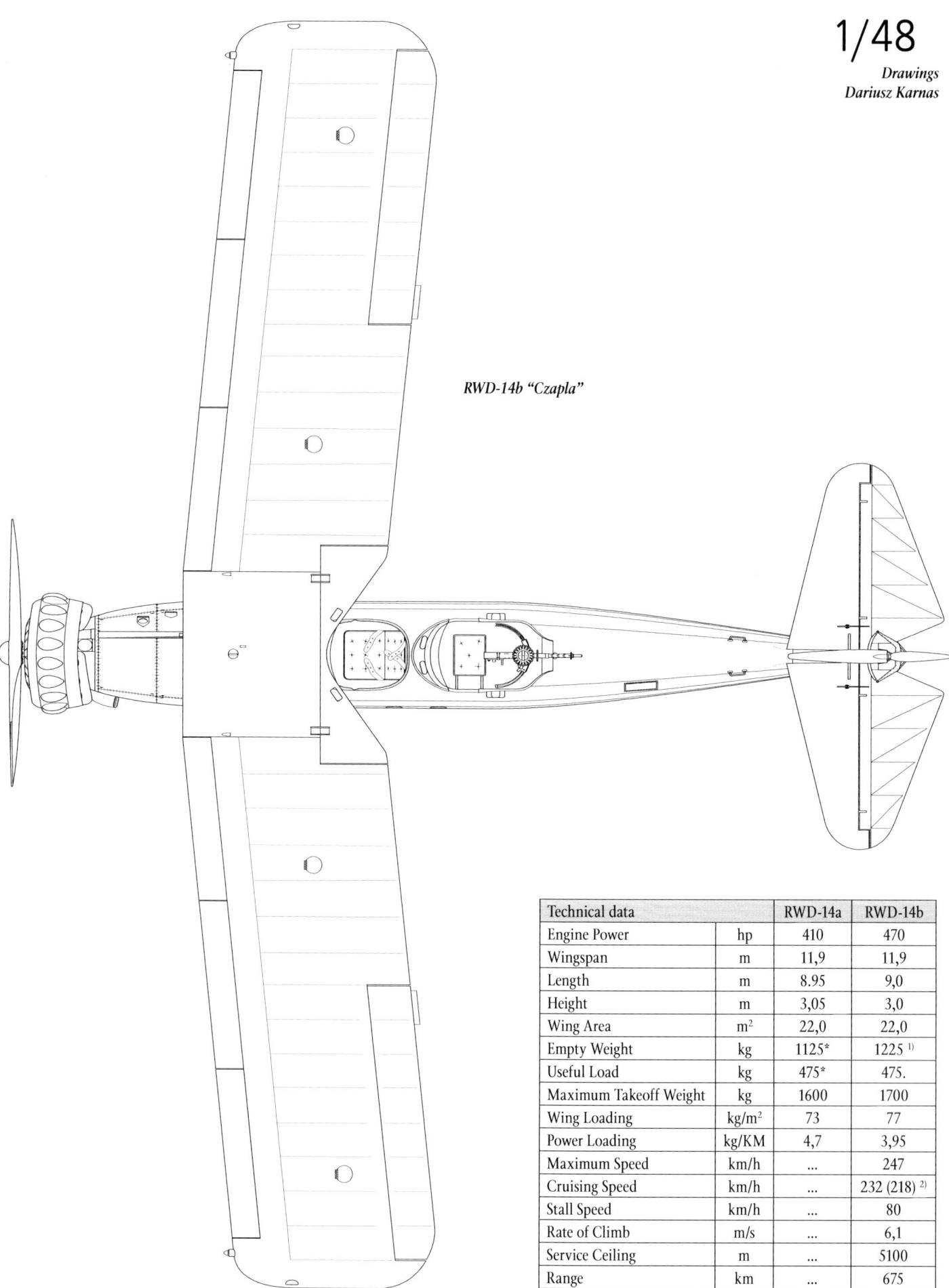

RWD-14b "Czapla"

Technical data		RWD-14a	RWD-14b
Engine Power	hp	410	470
Wingspan	m	11,9	11,9
Length	m	8.95	9,0
Height	m	3,05	3,0
Wing Area	m²	22,0	22,0
Empty Weight	kg	1125*	1225 [1]
Useful Load	kg	475*	475.
Maximum Takeoff Weight	kg	1600	1700
Wing Loading	kg/m²	73	77
Power Loading	kg/KM	4,7	3,95
Maximum Speed	km/h	...	247
Cruising Speed	km/h	...	232 (218) [2]
Stall Speed	km/h	...	80
Rate of Climb	m/s	...	6,1
Service Ceiling	m	...	5100
Range	km	...	675
Takeoff Run	m	...	140
Landing Roll	m	...	120

1) With armament (aircraft empty weight without removable equipment – 1153 kg)
2) At an altitude of 2100 m

1/48

Drawings
Dariusz Karnas

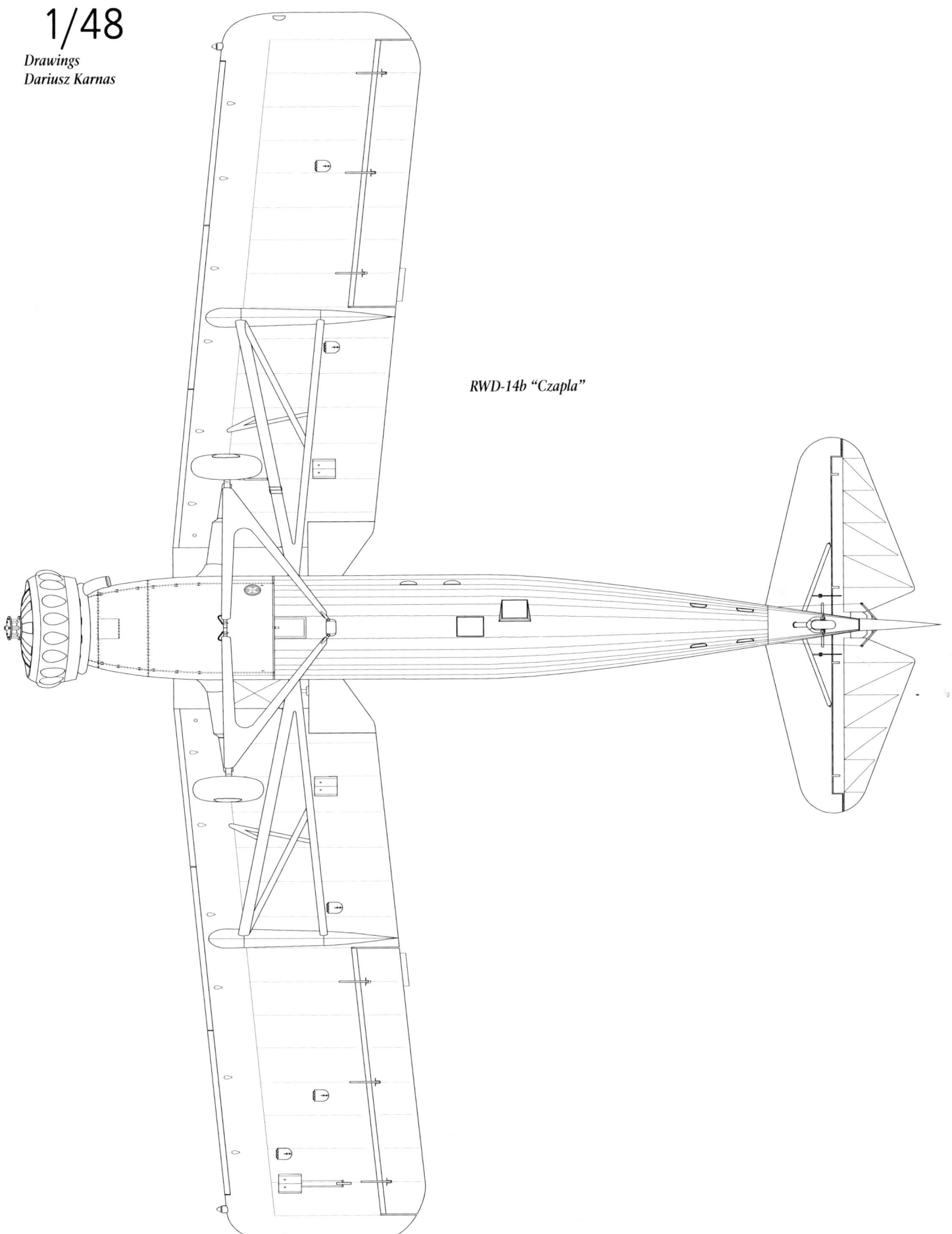

RWD-14b "Czapla"

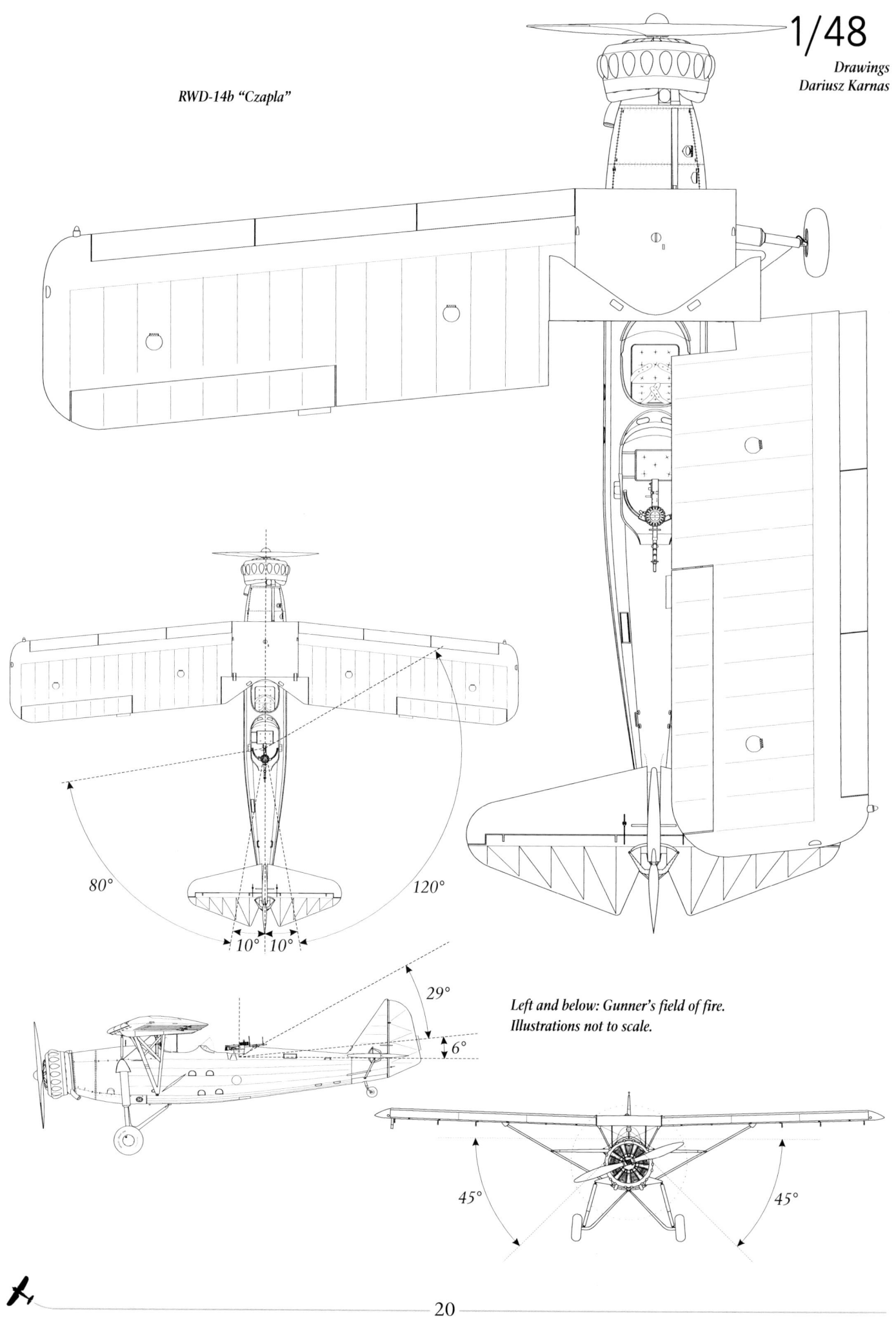

1/48

Drawings
Dariusz Karnas

RWD-14b "Czapla"

80°

120°

10° 10°

29°

6°

Left and below: Gunner's field of fire.
Illustrations not to scale.

45°

45°

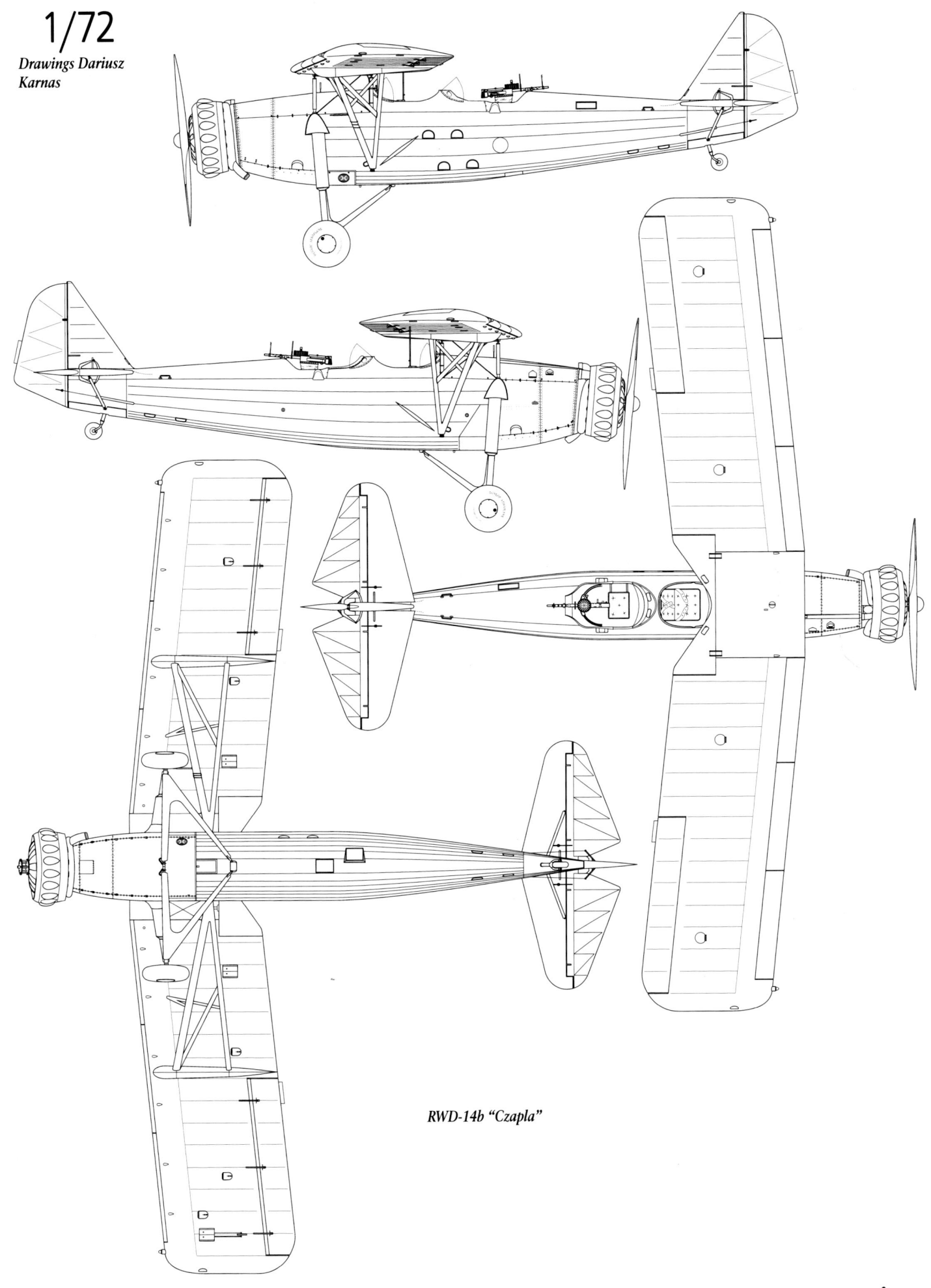

1/72
Drawings Dariusz Karnas

RWD-14b "Czapla"

Pilot's cockpit instrument panel.
Illustration by Dariusz Karnas.

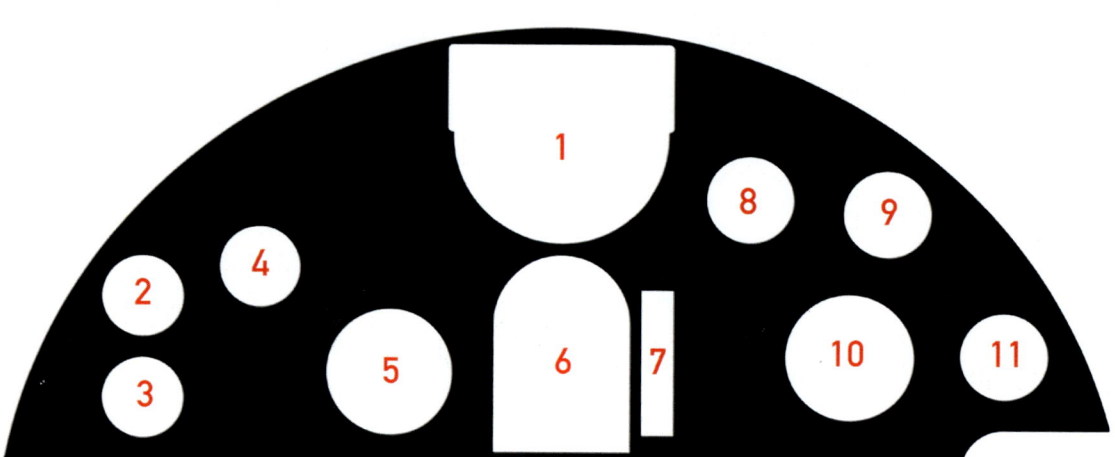

1. Magnetic compass;
2. Fuel pressure indicator;
3. Oil pressure indicator;
4. Oil temperature gauge;
5. Engine tachometer;
6. Integrated flight instrument (airspeed indicator, turn-and-slip indicator,

and attitude indicator);
7. Longitudinal attitude indicator;
8. Vertical speed indicator (VSI);
9. Chronometer;
10. Altimeter;
11. Fuel quantity indicator.

PZL G-1620B "Mors II" engine
with Szomański C.B.07 propeller
Scale 1/24

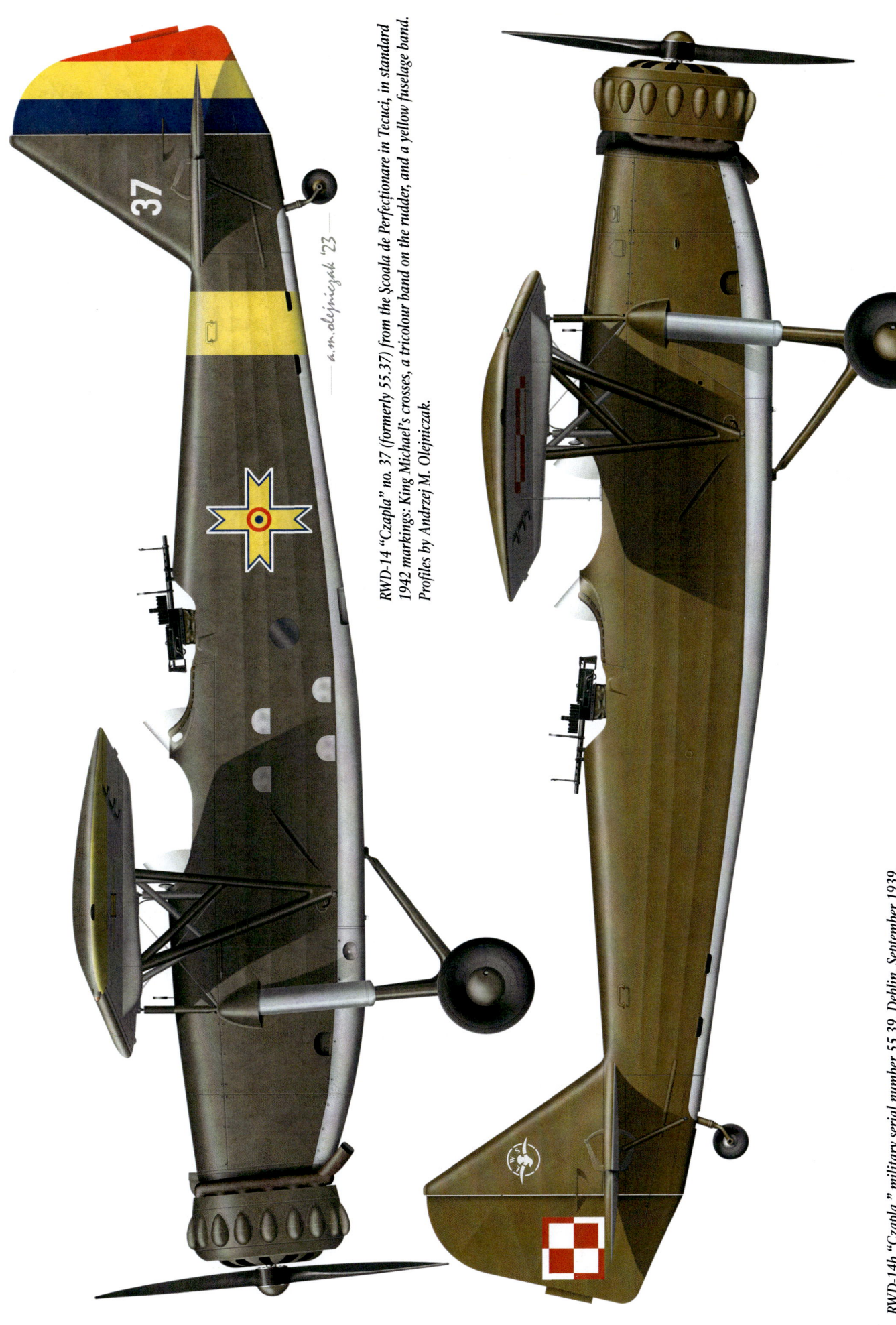

RWD-14 "Czapla" no. 37 (formerly 55.37) from the Şcoala de Perfecţionare in Tecuci, in standard 1942 markings: King Michael's crosses, a tricolour band on the rudder, and a yellow fuselage band. Profiles by Andrzej M. Olejniczak.

RWD-14b "Czapla," military serial number 55.39, Dęblin, September 1939. Upper surfaces of the aircraft in khaki, lower surfaces in silver. Profiles by Andrzej M. Olejniczak.

a.m.olejniczak '23

RWD-14b "Czapla," military serial number 55.39, Dęblin, September 1939.
Profiles by Andrzej M. Olejniczak.